GRID Perplexors

DEDUCTIVE LOGIC PUZZLES

MindWare®
brainy toys for kids of all ages®

www.MINDWAREonline.com

A MindWare® Original!

Our entire selection of Brainy Toys for Kids of All Ages® is available at www.MINDWAREonline.com, or by calling us at 800-999-0398 to request a catalog.

Coloring Books

Each of our coloring books offer one of a kind patterns, textures and styles you make your own by choosing how to bring them to life.

Animal Habitats Series

Creature Camouflage Series

Designs Series

Lights Series

Modern Patterns Series

Mosaics Series

Quilts Series

Scapes Series

Transformations Series

Puzzle Books

Our puzzle books build skills in many areas—from logic to math, spatial reasoning to verbal skills.

Addition Adventures

Analogy Challenges

Clip Clues

Code Breakers

Deducibles

Directive Detective

Division Designs

Fast Fact Trivia

Grid Perplexors

Logic Links

Math Path Puzzles

Math Perplexors

More Multiplication Mosaics

Multiplication Mosaics

Noodlers

Number Junctions

Perplexors

Sequencers

Subtraction Secrets

Tactic Twisters

Tan-Tastic Tangrams

Venn Perplexors

Word Winks

Word Wise

Games and Activities

Building blocks to strategic games, mystery puzzles to imaginative play — enhance abstract thinking and reasoning skills with our ingenious games and activities.

Bella's Mystery Decks

Blik-Blok

Block Buddies

Chaos

Cross-Eyed

Flip 4

Gambit

Hue Knew?

Logic Links Game

Make Your Own Mask Kit

Noodlers Game

Pattern Play

Qwirkle

Tally Rally

Squzzles

Configure nine 3 x 3 pieces into a square where all images match up on every single side. Three challenging puzzles per box.

3-D Scramblers

Animal Babies

Creature Kingdom

Creepy Crawlers

Illusions

Insect Infested

Nocturnal Animals

Optical Illusions

Play Ball!

Wings & Wheels

World Money

7/2007

© 2005 MindWare Holdings, Inc.

Individual Puzzles by Greg Gottstein
Design by Kristine Mudd

All rights reserved. Printed in the U.S.A.

Limited reproduction permission. The publisher grants permission to reproduce up to 100 copies of any part of this book for noncommercial classroom or individual use. Any further duplication is prohibited.

EAN 978-1-933054-07-0
SKU 26120

MindWare® brainy toys for kids of all ages®

for other MindWare products visit our website
www.MINDWAREonline.com

Instructions

When you are faced with a number of options, logic is often used to make a choice. Logic uses reasoning and proof to help you analyze information and come to a conclusion.

All the information needed to solve a Grid Perplexors logic problem is given in the puzzle story and its following clues. A solution grid provides a method of tracking the information deduced from the clues. Each empty box in the grid represents a "yes" or "no" possibility with each row in the grid containing exactly one "yes" answer.

THE STORY

Three cats named Tabby, Tommy and Terry were sitting in a tree. They either had white fur, brown fur, or black fur, and were wearing collars that were either red, pink or orange. Based on the clues, match the cat names with their fur and their collar colors.

THE CLUES

1. Tabby thought both the white cat and the cat in the pink collar had been rude to her.
2. Tommy did not wear a pink collar.
3. The brown cat wore a red collar.

	Tabby	Tommy	Terry
White Fur	X		
Brown Fur			
Black Fur			
Red Collar			
Pink Collar	X		
Orange Collar			

Clue one tells us that Tabby does not have white fur and does not wear a pink collar, so an "X" has been placed under Tabby's name indicating "no" for white fur and a pink collar. We also know that the white cat does not wear a pink collar, but cannot use this information yet.

	Tabby	Tommy	Terry
White Fur	X		X
Brown Fur			
Black Fur			
Red Collar			X
Pink Collar	X	X	O
Orange Collar			X

Clue two lets us eliminate the pink collar under Tommy with an "X," leaving Terry as the only cat who could be wearing pink, which we mark with an "O." Now we can also mark "X's" under Terry for the red and orange collars. The leftover information in clue one can now be used. Since Terry, as the pink collar-wearer, cannot have white fur, we can put another "X" onto the grid under Terry's name.

	Tabby	Tommy	Terry
White Fur	X	O	X
Brown Fur			
Black Fur			
Red Collar		X	X
Pink Collar	X	X	O
Orange Collar		O	X

Since neither Terry nor Tabby can have white fur, Tommy is the only cat who can be white, so we mark an "O" under his name. Clue three tells us that the brown cat wears a red collar, so we know that the white-furred Tommy cannot be wearing red, leaving orange as his only option. This in turn leaves the red collar as the only option for Tabby, who, again using clue three, must have brown fur. Finally, with white Tommy wearing the orange collar and brown Tabby wearing the red collar, the only option left for Terry with his pink collar is black fur.

© 2005 MindWare

1 Is Three Enough?

THE STORY

Three sisters from one family named Bess, Betty and Bertha married three brothers from another family named John, Jerry and Joe. The men's occupations were a barber, a fireman and a lawyer. Each of the married couples had one son and one daughter. The sons were named Bart, Bill and Bob, and the daughters were named Shana, Sheila and Sarah. Based on the clues, match the women with their husbands, their husband's occupations, their sons and their daughters.

THE CLUES

1. Sarah's father was a fireman, her Uncle Joe was a barber, and her cousin Shana's father was a lawyer.
2. Bertha was not married to Joe or the fireman.
3. Sheila's Aunt Bess was not married to a barber, and Bertha had a brother-in-law named John.
4. One of Bart's uncles was a fireman and the other was a lawyer.
5. Bess' favorite nephew was Bob.

	Bess	Betty	Bertha
John			
Jerry			
Joe			
Barber			
Fireman			
Lawyer			
Bart			
Bill			
Bob			
Shana			
Sheila			
Sarah			

 © 2005 MindWare

2 Playing Chicken

THE STORY

Three chickens named Henny, Penny and Jenny were best friends with a crow, a duck and a goose named Millie, Mary and Mattie. When the best friends got together, they enjoyed three different favorite activities. These favorite activities were watching TV, playing cards and telling stories. The best friends only had one serious disagreement. The subjects they disagreed over were egg raising, poetry and cooking. Based on the clues, match the chickens with the type of bird they were best friends with, the names of their best friends, their favorite activities, and the subjects of their only serious disagreement.

THE CLUES

1. Mattie was the card-playing crow.
2. Millie was a duck who loved to tell stories.
3. The goose loved to watch TV.
4. Penny had disagreed with her best friend over the subject of egg raising.
5. Jenny's best friend was not a goose, and she never disagreed over poetry.
6. Penny's best friend was not a goose, and she did not like to tell stories.

	Henny	Penny	Jenny
Crow			
Duck			
Goose			
Millie			
Mary			
Mattie			
Watching TV			
Playing cards			
Telling stories			
Egg raising			
Poetry			
Cooking			

3 Pond Life

THE STORY

Frank, Fran and Fred lived together in a large pond. They were a catfish, a bass and a carp. They weighed 2 pounds, 4 pounds and 5 pounds. They all had different favorite foods. Their favorite foods were crawfish, minnows and tadpoles. Thanks to unfortunate experiences with fishing lures, the fish all disliked different colors. The colors were red, orange and green. Based on the clues, match the fish with their species, their weights, their favorite foods and the colors they disliked.

THE CLUES

1. Fred weighed half as much as Frank.
2. The heaviest fish was not a bass, and the smallest fish was not a carp.
3. The bass loved to eat tadpoles and did not like red.
4. The carp loved to eat crawfish and did not like green.
5. Frank was not a bass, and Fran was not a carp.

	Frank	Fran	Fred
Catfish			
Bass			
Carp			
2 pounds			
4 pounds			
5 pounds			
Crawfish			
Minnows			
Tadpoles			
Red			
Orange			
Green			

 © 2005 MindWare

4 The Bike Ride

THE STORY

Walter, Wilma and Warren went on a long bike ride together. Their bicycles were different colors; they were red, orange and black. Oddly enough, they wore shirts that were red, orange and black, but none of them wore a shirt that was the same color as their bike. Along the way, they stopped for something to eat and ordered a hot dog, a hamburger and a taco. To wash their food down, they ordered root beer, iced tea and lemonade. Based on the clues, match the names with their bicycle colors, their shirt colors, their food choices and their drinks.

THE CLUES

1. None of the children's bicycle colors matched their shirt colors.
2. Wilma's bike was not orange or black, and Warren's shirt was not red or black.
3. The child in the black shirt ate a taco and drank root beer.
4. The child on the black bike did not order a hot dog.
5. The child wearing a red shirt did not order iced tea.

	Walter	Wilma	Warren
Red bike			
Orange bike			
Black bike			
Red shirt			
Orange shirt			
Black shirt			
Hot dog			
Hamburger			
Taco			
Root beer			
Iced tea			
Lemonade			

© 2005 MindWare

5 Fun In The Park

THE STORY

Four children named Ken, Keith, Kathy and Kate decided to spend the day in the park. For lunch, they each brought a different item: bologna, bread, mustard and lemonade. They all wore shoes of different colors. The shoes were pink, yellow, purple and white. All the children were stung by a different insect. The insects were a wasp, a hornet, a bee and a yellow jacket. When they were stung, they all shouted something different. They shouted "yowzer," "mommy," "drat" and "jeepers." Based on the clues, match the children with their lunch items, their shoe colors, the insects that stung them and what they shouted.

THE CLUES

1. The child in the purple shoes, who brought the bologna, shouted "drat" when stung by a yellow jacket.
2. The child who shouted "jeepers" when stung by the hornet wore pink shoes and brought the mustard.
3. Ken and Kate never wore anything pink or purple.
4. Kathy thought "drat" was not a good expression.
5. The child stung by the wasp shouted "yowzer" and wore white shoes.
6. Ken did not bring the lemonade, and his shoes were not white.

	Ken	Keith	Kathy	Kate
Bologna				
Bread				
Mustard				
Lemonade				
Pink shoes				
Yellow shoes				
Purple shoes				
White shoes				
Wasp				
Hornet				
Bee				
Yellow jacket				
"Yowzer"				
"Mommy"				
"Drat"				
"Jeepers"				

 © 2005 MindWare

6 Breakfast Food

THE STORY

Four sales representatives named Victor, Val, Virginia and Vinnie went to four different restaurants for breakfast. The restaurants were the Cozy Cup, the Stanley Cup, the Tea Cup and the Coffee Cup. They all ordered omelets, but each ordered a different kind of omelet. They ordered a ham omelet, an onion omelet, a cheese omelet and a bacon omelet. Being big eaters, they also ordered pancakes, waffles, French toast and crepes. Their beverages were coffee, tea, milk and tomato juice. Based on the clues, match the sales people with their restaurants, their choice of omelets, their additional orders and their beverages.

THE CLUES

1. Virginia and Vinnie did not drink either milk or tomato juice.
2. The milk drinker ate an onion omelet and pancakes at the Tea Cup restaurant.
3. The tea drinker ate a ham omelet and crepes at the Cozy Cup restaurant.
4. The tomato juice drinker ate a cheese omelet and waffles at the Stanley Cup restaurant.
5. Virginia did not eat at the Cozy Cup restaurant, and Val did not eat at the Stanley Cup restaurant.

	Victor	Val	Virginia	Vinnie
Cozy Cup				
Stanley Cup				
Tea Cup				
Coffee Cup				
Ham				
Onion				
Cheese				
Bacon				
Pancakes				
Waffles				
French toast				
Crepes				
Coffee				
Tea				
Milk				
Tomato juice				

© 2005 MindWare

7 Sinking Ships

THE STORY

Four ship captains named Captain Hoover, Captain Adams, Captain Ford and Captain Johnson lost their ships in storms. The ships were the Sea Sprite, the Sea Witch, the Sea Belle and the Sea Otter. The storms that sank the ships were a hurricane, a typhoon, a tornado and a blizzard. None of the members of the crew were lost on any ship, and 10 sailors were saved on one ship, 20 on another, 25 on the third and 30 on the fourth. Oddly enough, the crew survived on lifeboats for 10 days, 20 days, 25 days and 30 days, but in no case did the number of crew members saved and the number of days in a lifeboat match. Based on the clues, match the captains with their ships, the storms that sank the ships, the number of crew members saved, and the number of days they survived on lifeboats.

THE CLUES

1. The number of crew members saved did not ever match the number of days spent in a lifeboat.
2. Neither Captain Hoover nor Captain Adams lost their ships in a hurricane or a typhoon.
3. The Sea Witch was lost during a tornado, and the Sea Otter was lost during a blizzard.
4. The Sea Sprite had twice as many sailors as the Sea Belle, and the Sea Belle's crew was on a lifeboat twice as many days as the Sea Sprite's crew.
5. Captain Hoover was not the captain of the Sea Otter that was lost during a blizzard, and he did not spend the most time in a lifeboat.
6. Captain Ford spent more time in a lifeboat than the captain of the Sea Sprite that sank during a hurricane.

	Captain Hoover	Captain Adams	Captain Ford	Captain Johnson
Sea Sprite				
Sea Witch				
Sea Belle				
Sea Otter				
Hurricane				
Typhoon				
Tornado				
Blizzard				
10 sailors				
20 sailors				
25 sailors				
30 sailors				
10 days				
20 days				
25 days				
30 days				

 © 2005 MindWare

8 Yachts of Luck

THE STORY

Zeke, Zelda, Zoe and Zach decided to enter an around-the-world yacht race. The names of their yachts were Flyer, Speedy, Ripper and Demon. None of them traveled very far before they were forced to drop out of the race. They sailed 6 miles, 12 miles, 13 miles and 15 miles before disaster struck. One yacht hit a rock, another broke a rudder, another broke a mast, and the fourth sprung a leak. Repair costs for the yachts were $10,000, $20,000, $21,000 and $22,000. Based on the clues, match the yacht owners with their yachts, the distances they traveled, the disasters that befell them, and the costs to repair their yachts.

THE CLUES

1. Zoe sailed twice as far as Zach, but Zeke sailed the farthest.
2. Zeke and Zelda did not hit a rock or spring a leak, but their repairs were the most expensive.
3. Flyer and Demon were the cheapest to repair.
4. Zach spent half as much as the owner of Flyer, whose yacht sprung a leak.
5. Zeke spent less than the owner of Speedy that broke a rudder.

	Zeke	Zelda	Zoe	Zach
Flyer				
Speedy				
Ripper				
Demon				
6 miles				
12 miles				
13 miles				
15 miles				
Hit a rock				
Broken rudder				
Broken mast				
Sprung a leak				
$10,000				
$20,000				
$21,000				
$22,000				

9 Don't Buy It

THE STORY

Edith, Elmo, Eddie and Ellen recently went to auctions at four different auction houses: Al's Auctions, Bea's Auctions, Cal's Auctions and Don's Auctions. They all bid on and won one item. The items were a bed warmer, a chair, a painting and a desk. At one time, the items belonged to a prince, a duke, an earl and a dame. The winning bids were $25, $50, $62 and $64. Based on the clues, match the names with the auction houses, the items won, the previous owners and the winning bid amounts.

THE CLUES

1. Alphabetically speaking, Elmo's auction house starts with a letter that immediately precedes Edith's auction house, but Ellen's auction house starts with a letter that precedes all the others except, of course, for Eddie's auction house.
2. The duke's velvet horse painting went for the second highest amount.
3. Eddie spent twice as much as Elmo, and neither one bought the dame's chair, which was the most expensive item.
4. Ellen spent more than Edith, and the earl's desk cost the least.

	Edith	Elmo	Eddie	Ellen
Al's Auctions				
Bea's Auctions				
Cal's Auctions				
Don's Auctions				
Bed warmer				
Chair				
Painting				
Desk				
Prince				
Duke				
Earl				
Dame				
$25				
$50				
$62				
$64				

 © 2005 MindWare

10 Executives

THE STORY

Joan, Jim, Josh and Jean were the heads of important departments at the Widget Corporation. The departments were sales, shipping, production and accounting. They had different numbers of employees under their direction. They had 100 employees, 150 employees, 200 employees and 300 employees. The executives were different ages. They were 30 years old, 34 years old, 39 years old and 60 years old. One of their responsibilities was to hand out gold watches to employees who retired from their departments. Last year, they handed out 3 gold watches, 6 gold watches, 9 gold watches and 12 gold watches. Based on the clues, match the executives with the departments they headed, the number of their employees, their ages, and the number of gold watches they handed out.

THE CLUES

1. Josh directed twice as many employees as Jim but fewer than Jean.
2. The oldest executive directed twice as many employees as Joan.
3. Joan and Jim had nothing to do with sales or shipping, which were directed by the youngest and oldest executives.
4. Jim, who had nothing to do with accounting, handed out half as many gold watches as the 39-year-old accountant.
5. The executive in charge of shipping handed out the most gold watches.
6. Jean was not responsible for sales.

	Joan	Jim	Josh	Jean
Sales				
Shipping				
Production				
Accounting				
100 employees				
150 employees				
200 employees				
300 employees				
30 years old				
34 years old				
39 years old				
60 years old				
3 gold watches				
6 gold watches				
9 gold watches				
12 gold watches				

11 First Ladies

THE STORY

Four females named Connie, Cathy, Carol and Callie lived in the small town of Harden. Their last names were Fuller, Frye, Fowler and Farley. They all were celebrating important firsts in their lives. These firsts were first job, first marriage, first baby and first birthday. They had four different eye colors; they were blue, black, brown and green. Oddly enough, their hair colors were also blue, black, brown and green, but nobody had the same color for both eyes and hair. Based on the clues, match the first names with their last names, their important firsts, their eye colors and their hair colors.

THE CLUES

1. No female had the same color eyes and hair.
2. Fuller was the youngest, Frye was starting her first job, and Cathy was getting married.
3. Connie had worked as a secretary before starting her present job, and Carol was not a baby.
4. Cathy and Carol did not have black eyes, green eyes, blue hair or brown hair.
5. Frye's eyes were not brown, and Fowler's hair was black.
6. The baby had green eyes, and Farley's hair was not blue.

	Connie	Cathy	Carol	Callie
Fuller				
Frye				
Fowler				
Farley				
First job				
First marriage				
First baby				
First birthday				
Blue eyes				
Black eyes				
Brown eyes				
Green eyes				
Blue hair				
Black hair				
Brown hair				
Green hair				

 © 2005 MindWare

12 Late for School

THE STORY

Dan, Diana, Donna and Del whose last names were Adams, Jefferson, Madison and Monroe, were late for school on different days of the week. One was late on Monday, another on Tuesday, another on Thursday and still another on Friday. They were students in the 5th, 6th, 7th and 8th grades. Their excuses were overslept, power outage, missed the bus, and forgot it was a school day. Based on the clues, match the first names with their last names, the days of the week they were late, the grades they were in and their excuses.

THE CLUES

1. Adams was late earlier in the week than Jefferson and Monroe, but not before Madison.
2. The 5th grader and the 7th grader were tardy later in the week than the other two students.
3. Dan and Diana were in the highest grades, and neither one claimed to have missed the bus or forgot it was a school day.
4. Donna was in a lower grade than Del, and Dan was in a higher grade than Diana.
5. Diana was tardy earlier in the week than Donna, and Dan who did not say he overslept, was tardy later in the week than Del.
6. Del did not say he missed the bus because that was Monroe's excuse.

	Dan	Diana	Donna	Del
Adams				
Jefferson				
Madison				
Monroe				
Monday				
Tuesday				
Thursday				
Friday				
5th grade				
6th grade				
7th grade				
8th grade				
Overslept				
Power outage				
Missed bus				
Forgot				

13 Frog Kissing Perils

THE STORY

Recently, five peasants named Will, Walt, Warren, Winston and Weston went to a local swamp and kissed as many frogs as possible in the hopes that one of them would turn into a princess. Frogs are hard to catch, but the peasants managed to kiss 8 frogs, 12 frogs, 16 frogs, 22 frogs and 24 frogs. Five witches named Hortense, Harriet, Hilda, Helga and Helveta, who co-owned the swamp, came upon the peasants kissing their frogs and became incensed at the unseemly displays of affection. To show their displeasure, the witches each chose a different peasant and turned him into an animal. The animals were a newt, a goat, a skink, a vole and a gopher. Based on the clues, match the peasants with the number of frogs they kissed, the witches that turned them into animals, and the animals they were turned into.

THE CLUES

1. Walt was not turned into a goat, and Warren was not turned into anything by Helveta.
2. Weston and Winston kissed the most frogs.
3. Harriet and Helga changed the peasant who kissed the most frogs and the peasant who kissed the fewest frogs into a skink and a gopher.
4. Will kissed half as many frogs as Walt, but Winston kissed twice as many frogs as Warren.
5. Hortense, Helga and Helveta changed the three peasants who kissed the fewest frogs into a goat, a vole and a gopher.

	Will	Walt	Warren	Winston	Weston
8 frogs					
12 frogs					
16 frogs					
22 frogs					
24 frogs					
Hortense					
Harriet					
Hilda					
Helga					
Helveta					
Newt					
Goat					
Skink					
Vole					
Gopher					

 © 2005 MindWare

14 Walking Robins

THE STORY

During the summers, five robins named Frank, Farah, Fran, Farley and Frieda lived in Chicago, Toledo, Detroit, New York and Albany. One year, when it came time to fly to Mexico for the winter, they all got it into their heads to walk instead of fly! Where they got this idea no one knows. They all walked different distances before deciding that walking to Mexico was a bad idea. They walked 2, 4, 5, 6 and 8 miles before giving up on the walking idea and flying the rest of the way to Mexico. They all spent the winter in different Mexican cities: Acapulco, Mexicali, Oaxaca, Tijuana and Tampico. Based on the clues, match the names with the cities where they spent the summer, the distances they walked, and the Mexican cities where they spent the winter.

THE CLUES

1. Frank walked twice as far as Farah, and Farah walked twice as far as Fran, and Frieda walked farther than Farley.
2. The Chicago robin walked twice as far as the Toledo robin, and the Toledo robin walked twice as far as the New York robin, and the Detroit robin did not walk as far as the Albany robin.
3. The robins from Detroit, New York and Albany flew to Acapulco, Mexicali and Oaxaca.
4. The robin that walked the farthest ended up flying to Tijuana.
5. The robin that walked the shortest distance flew to Acapulco, and the Detroit robin did not fly to Oaxaca.

	Frank	Farah	Fran	Farley	Frieda
Chicago					
Toledo					
Detroit					
New York					
Albany					
2 miles					
4 miles					
5 miles					
6 miles					
8 miles					
Acapulco					
Mexicali					
Oaxaca					
Tijuana					
Tampico					

15 Fast Food Logic

THE STORY

Five friends named Greg, Gail, Gaylord, Gina and George were standing in line at a snack shop. They were 1st, 2nd, 3rd, 4th and 5th in line, and they ordered a hot dog, a burger, a taco, a gyro and a bratwurst. To drink, they ordered cola, lemonade, tea, coffee and milk. Based on the clues, match the friends with their places in line, the food they ordered and the drinks they ordered.

THE CLUES

1. The taco was washed down with a cola.
2. The lemonade was ordered after the burger and tea combination were ordered, but before the hot dog and coffee combination were ordered.
3. The last three people in line did not order either cola or milk.
4. Gina took a step back and stepped on Gail's toes, causing Gail to step back and step on Greg's toes, causing Greg to step back and step on Gaylord's toes, causing Gaylord to step back, but nobody was behind him so he did not step on any toes.
5. The taco was ordered after the bratwurst was ordered, but the hot dog, burger and gyro were all ordered after the taco was ordered.

	Greg	Gail	Gaylord	Gina	George
1st in line					
2nd in line					
3rd in line					
4th in line					
5th in line					
Hot dog					
Burger					
Taco					
Gyro					
Bratwurst					
Cola					
Lemonade					
Tea					
Coffee					
Milk					

 © 2005 MindWare

16 June Birthdays

THE STORY

Edward, Ellie, Eilene, Ennis and Elsbeth, whose last names were Funk, Fritz, Flynn, Freese and Fisher had consecutive birthdays in the month of June. Their birthdays were June 6th, June 7th, June 8th, June 9th and June 10th. They were not were born in the same year, so they were all different ages. They were 10, 15, 20, 30 and 40 years old. Based on the clues, match the first and last names, the day in June on which they were born and their ages.

THE CLUES

1. Eilene's birthday was later than Ennis' birthday, Flynn was the oldest of the group, and Freese was the youngest.
2. Elsbeth was younger than Ellie, and Ennis was older than Eilene.
3. Edward's age was twice as large as his birth date, and Edward, by the way, was not Funk.
4. Multiply Ellie's birth date by five and you get her age but, of course, you can do the same thing to Elsbeth's birth date to arrive at Elsbeth's age.
5. Flynn and Fisher were older than Edward, Eilene and Ennis.

	Edward	Ellie	Eilene	Ennis	Elsbeth
Funk					
Fritz					
Flynn					
Freese					
Fisher					
June 6th					
June 7th					
June 8th					
June 9th					
June 10th					
10 years old					
15 years old					
20 years old					
30 years old					
40 years old					

© 2005 MindWare

17 Fastest Pecking Awards

THE STORY

Five birds named Becky, Billy, Bobby, Benny and Betsy were very competitive and were constantly engaging in different contests. The birds were a chicken, a turkey, a duck, a goose and a pigeon. One day, they decided to hold a pecking contest to see which one of them could peck the most times in one minute. The results were 40 pecks, 60 pecks, 80 pecks, 100 pecks, and an impressive 150 pecks. The birds pecked so enthusiastically that they actually injured themselves slightly. The injuries they suffered were a bent beak, a headache, neck strain, crossed-eyes and ringing ears. Based on the clues, match the names with their bird types, the number of pecks and their slight injuries.

THE CLUES

1. The goose pecked itself cross-eyed, the chicken bent its beak, and the turkey had a headache.
2. The chicken pecked much faster than the pigeon, the duck out-pecked the goose, and the goose out-pecked the turkey.
3. Billy pecked faster than Bobby and Benny, but Becky pecked faster than Billy.
4. The turkey, the duck and the goose were not the fastest pecker or the slowest pecker, and none of them suffered from either a bent beak or from ringing in their ears.
5. Benny and Betsy were the chicken and the pigeon, but maybe not in that order.

	Becky	Billy	Bobby	Benny	Betsy
Chicken					
Turkey					
Duck					
Goose					
Pigeon					
40 pecks					
60 pecks					
80 pecks					
100 pecks					
150 pecks					
Bent beak					
Headache					
Neck strain					
Crossed-eyes					
Ringing ears					

 © 2005 MindWare

18 School Awards

THE STORY

Kate, Ken, Karen, Kyle and Knute whose last names were Kempe, Kelly, Kersey, Knapper and Knoll were all recipients of the Kingsford School's annual academic awards. The awards were granted in the subject areas of French, math, English, science and logic. The awards were granted based on the highest percentage scores in that particular subject. This year, the winning percentages were 100%, 99%, 98%, 97% and 96%. Based on the clues, match the first and last names, the subject areas in which the students won their awards, and their percentage scores for that subject.

THE CLUES

1. Kersey's winning percentage was not the highest.
2. Kyle's score was lower than Karen's score, but higher than Kelly's winning score in logic.
3. Kate and Ken were Kempe and Knoll, won prizes in French and math, and had the lowest scores.
4. The science award was based on a 100% winning percentage, and the lowest score earning a prize was in French and, oddly enough, Kempe did not have the lowest score because Ken had that distinction.

	Kate	Ken	Karen	Kyle	Knute
Kempe					
Kelly					
Kersey					
Knapper					
Knoll					
French					
Math					
English					
Science					
Logic					
100%					
99%					
98%					
97%					
96%					

© 2005 MindWare

19

Basketball Team Logic

THE STORY

The starting five players on the Blueberry Hill High School basketball team were Norm, Nate, Neil, Nigel and Niles. Their last names were Nabors, Napton, Nesbitt, Nolan and Nielsen. The numbers on their team uniforms were 5, 7, 10, 15 and 20 and, oddly enough, their points per game averages were 5, 7, 10, 15 and 20 points. Even more odd was the fact that three of the uniform numbers exactly matched three of the points per game average numbers! Based on the clues, match the first and last names, the uniform numbers, and the points per game average numbers.

THE CLUES

1. Three of the numbers on the uniforms exactly match three of the average points per game numbers.
2. Nesbitt had the highest points per game average, Napton's uniform number was half as large as Nesbitt's uniform number, Nabors' uniform number and points per game numbers matched, and Nielsen wore the smallest uniform number.
3. Nigel's uniform number was half as large as Norm's uniform number, and Norm's points per game average was twice as large as Niles' points per game average.
4. Norm did not have the largest number on his uniform, and he did not have the largest points per game average either.
5. Neil's points per game average was twice as large as Norm's points per game average, and Nate's points per game average was higher than Norm's points per game average.

	Norm	Nate	Neil	Nigel	Niles
Nabors					
Napton					
Nesbitt					
Nolan					
Nielsen					
#5					
#7					
#10					
#15					
#20					
5 points					
7 points					
10 points					
15 points					
20 points					

 © 2005 MindWare

20 Tearful Movie

THE STORY

Billy, Bob, Bert, Brenda and Barb all watched the saddest movie ever. Their last names were Dray, Drew, Driscoll, Driver and Durley. They enjoyed the movie so much that they all saw it many times, but no two movie-goers saw it the same number of times. They watched the movie 12, 18, 24, 36, or an incredible 72 times. They always cried during each showing of the movie but. of course, no two movie-goers cried the same number of gallons of tears. They cried 6, 9, 12, 20 or 24 gallons. Based on the clues, match the first and last names, the number of times they watched the movie, and the number of gallons of tears they cried.

THE CLUES

1. Dray did not see the movie 36 times, and Durley cried more gallons than Dray.
2. Drew saw the movie the most times but, oddly enough, cried the fewest gallons.
3. Driver saw the movie twice as many times as Billy, which means the number of times Driver saw the movie is twice as large as the number of gallons he cried.
4. The number of gallons in Driscoll's tear production is twice as large as the number of times he saw the movie.
5. Bob thought Driver never understood the movie, Driscoll was just a big crybaby, and Drew did not cry enough based on the emotion of that movie.
6. Brenda thought Drew cried too much, Driscoll was too sensitive, and Driver was not sensitive enough.
7. Bob was not Durley, and Barb was not Driscoll or Driver, and Bert, of course, saw the movie more than 12 times.

	Billy	Bob	Bert	Brenda	Barb
Dray					
Drew					
Driscoll					
Driver					
Durley					
12 times					
18 times					
24 times					
36 times					
72 times					
6 gallons					
9 gallons					
12 gallons					
20 gallons					
24 gallons					

© 2005 MindWare

21 Mexican Food Mix-Up

THE STORY

Charlie Wang, a logic-loving owner of a Mexican restaurant offered luncheon specials Monday through Friday. But the menu he posted for the week was always completely wrong, and Charlie offered clues to his logical customers so they would know what the luncheon specials really were for that week. Shown below is Charlie's completely wrong menu for a recent week.

	Main Dish	Side Dish	Beverage
Monday	Tacos	Rice	Cola
Tuesday	Burritos	Beans	Lemonade
Wednesday	Enchiladas	Salad	Iced tea
Thursday	Tamales	Potatoes	Coffee
Friday	Tostadas	Nachos	Root beer

Based on the clues, figure out Charlie Wang's real menu for the week, or you can just go home for lunch and forget it.

THE CLUES

1. Not only is the menu to the left completely wrong, but also the combinations are completely wrong as nothing was served together as shown.
2. On Monday, Charlie said, "Today's real main dish is Thursday's main dish according to the menu, tomorrow's real main dish is the day after Thursday's main dish according to the menu, and the day after tomorrow's real main dish is what the menu says I will be serving tomorrow."
3. Ever helpful that Monday, Charlie added, "Today's side dish is tomorrow's side dish, and tomorrow's real side dish is today's side dish according to the menu."
4. Charlie's final advice on Monday was, "Today, I'm really serving the day after tomorrow's beverage according to the menu."

	Monday	Tuesday	Wednesday	Thursday	Friday
Tacos					
Burritos					
Enchiladas					
Tamales					
Tostadas					
Rice					
Beans					
Salad					
Potatoes					
Nachos					
Cola					
Lemonade					
Iced tea					
Coffee					
Root beer					

 © 2005 MindWare

22 School Organization

THE STORY

Five teachers named Alice, Bert, Carol, David and Elwood worked at the same school. Their last names were Smith, Smythe, Schmit, Smolt and Schultz. Their classrooms were 102, 103, 104, 105 and 106, and they taught 2nd, 3rd, 4th, 5th and 6th grades. The teachers decided that they were all in the wrong rooms, and after many meetings, they decided that the rooms should be assigned based on the alphabetical order of their first names. According to the new plan, the person whose first name began with the letter furthest from the beginning of the alphabet would be assigned to the room with the lowest number. Therefore, Elwood would be assigned to 102, David would be assigned to 103, and so on until Alice would be assigned to 106. Based on the clues, match the first and last names, the rooms that the teachers were in before the new plan was implemented, and the grades they taught.

THE CLUES

1. According to the new plan of assigning rooms based on alphabetical privilege, the teachers were all now in the wrong rooms.
2. Schultz had taught 4th grade in Room 104, and Elwood would be moving to Smith's room once the new plan took effect.
3. Alice thought Schmit, the 3rd grade teacher from Room 103, was too permissive with the students compared to the way she disciplined her younger students.
4. Bert, of course, did not teach 5th grade, and his name was not Smolt.
5. Alice, Carol and David were not named Smith or Smolt, and they did not teach the two highest grades shown.

	Alice	Bert	Carol	David	Elwood
Smith					
Smythe					
Schmit					
Smolt					
Schultz					
Room 102					
Room 103					
Room 104					
Room 105					
Room 106					
2nd grade					
3rd grade					
4th grade					
5th grade					
6th grade					

© 2005 MindWare

23 Picnic In The Park

THE STORY

Five children named Helga, Henry, Helen, Harvey and Harold decided to have a picnic in the park. They all agreed to bring one food item and one drink item. For food, they brought hot dogs, bread, pickles, apples and donuts. The drinks they brought were cola, lemonade, iced tea, root beer and fruit punch. The children all had different colored bicycles that they rode to the park. The bicycles were, red, white, blue, green and pink. Based on the clues, match the children with their food items, their drinks and their bicycle colors.

THE CLUES

1. Helga and Henry did not ride a red, white or pink bike, and they did not bring cola, lemonade or iced tea.
2. Helen, Harvey and Harold did not bring hot dogs or bread to the picnic.
3. Helga did not bring hot dogs or ride a green bike.
4. The child on the green bike did not bring root beer.
5. Helen did not bring apples or lemonade, and her bike was not white.
6. Harvey thought the children who brought the pickles and donuts rode their white and pink bikes well.
7. The child with the red bike brought lemonade.
8. The child with the pink bike brought iced tea, but did not bring the donuts.

	Helga	Henry	Helen	Harvey	Harold
Hot dogs					
Bread					
Pickles					
Apples					
Donuts					
Cola					
Lemonade					
Iced tea					
Root beer					
Fruit punch					
Red bike					
White bike					
Blue bike					
Green bike					
Pink bike					

 © 2005 MindWare

24 Howl Do You Like It?

THE STORY

Five dogs named Jack, Jane, Judy, Jill and Jimmy decided to hold a contest to see who could howl the longest without taking a breath. The dogs howled for 20 seconds, 30 seconds, 40 seconds, 45 seconds and 60 seconds. Aside from howling, the dogs had other interests. They all liked chasing things. They liked to chase cats, cars, squirrels, mice and birds. The dogs were different breeds. They were a beagle, a poodle, a terrier, a collie and an elkhound. Based on the clues, match the dogs with their longest howl, what they liked to chase and their breeds.

THE CLUES

1. Jill and Jimmy liked to chase cats and cars, and howled for the shortest time and the longest time, but maybe not in that order.
2. Jack and Jane agreed that the terrier, collie and elkhound had a terrible bad breath problem.
3. Jill howled less than Jimmy, and Jimmy, who did not chase cats, howled twice as long as Judy.
4. Jack was afraid of squirrels and birds and never chased them, and Jack also howled less than Jane.
5. The beagle chased birds.
6. The terrier chased squirrels, and the elkhound chased cats.

	Jack	Jane	Judy	Jill	Jimmy
20 seconds					
30 seconds					
40 seconds					
45 seconds					
60 seconds					
Cats					
Cars					
Squirrels					
Mice					
Birds					
Beagle					
Poodle					
Terrier					
Collie					
Elkhound					

© 2005 MindWare

25 Baseball Players

THE STORY

Five children named Clara, Charles, Cathy, Cindi and Clark played together on the same baseball team. Their positions were 1st base, 2nd base, 3rd base, left field and right field. Their uniform numbers were 2, 3, 4, 9 and 18. After one recent game, they went out for ice cream together, and they all ordered a different flavor. They ordered vanilla, chocolate, strawberry, lemon and banana. Based on the clues, match the children with their team positions, their uniform numbers and their ice cream flavors.

THE CLUES

1. Charles' uniform number was twice as large as Cathy's uniform number, but Cindi's uniform number was larger than Charles' uniform number and was twice as large as Clark's uniform number.
2. The children with the two highest uniform numbers did not play any of the bases.
3. The left fielder and the right fielder ordered the vanilla and banana ice cream.
4. The child with the highest uniform number did not play right field or order banana ice cream.
5. Charles' position in the field was between the children who ordered chocolate and lemon ice cream.
6. Cathy did not play 3rd base, and she hated lemon ice cream.

	Clara	Charles	Cathy	Cindi	Clark
1st base					
2nd base					
3rd base					
Left field					
Right field					
# 2					
# 3					
# 4					
# 9					
# 18					
Vanilla					
Chocolate					
Strawberry					
Lemon					
Banana					

 © 2005 MindWare

26 Logical Lunch

THE STORY

Every week, the Logic Café changed its menu and wrote logic clues for the customers so they could figure out what the daily lunch special was. This week, the menu announced that the menu as shown below was completely wrong. All the main courses were incorrect, all the vegetables were incorrect, and all the beverages were incorrect. Based on the clues and the menu, see if you can figure out the lunch specials for each day of the week.

Mon.	Tues.	Wed.	Thurs.	Fri.
Meat loaf	Fish	Hamburger	Ham	Pot roast
Spinach	Potatoes	Beets	Cabbage	Carrots
Milk	Coffee	Cola	Tea	Lemonade

THE CLUES

1. All of the ma n courses, vegetables and beverages as shown on the menu are wrong.
2. On Monday, the clue for the main course deductions said, "Today's main course is really tomorrow's main course, and tomorrow's main course is really today's main course, but Wednesday's main course will really be served on Friday."
3. On Monday, the clue for the vegetables read, "Today's vegetable will be served tomorrow, but tomorrow's vegetable will be served the day after tomorrow, while Friday's vegetable will really be served on Thursday, and Thursday's vegetable will really be served on Friday."
4. On Monday, the clues for the beverages read, "Today's beverage will really be served on Thursday, tomorrow's beverage will really be served on the day after tomorrow, tea will not be served on Friday, and lemonade will not be served tomorrow."

	Monday	Tuesday	Wednesday	Thursday	Friday
Meat loaf					
Fish					
Hamburger					
Ham					
Pot roast					
Spinach					
Potatoes					
Beets					
Cabbage					
Carrots					
Milk					
Coffee					
Cola					
Tea					
Lemonade					

27 Mountain Climbing

THE STORY

Five children named Bonnie, Blake, Blair, Billy and Bert were members of the same family and they were all born at different times. This meant that one was born first, another second, and so on. The children decided to race to the top of Mt. Baldy. They all made it to the top, but one child was first to the top, another was second to the top, and so on. When they reached the top, they all said something different. They said "I'm tired," "whew," "made it," "wow" and "never again." Based on the clues, match the children with their birth order, their order of finish, and what they said at the top of the mountain.

THE CLUES

1. None of the children's orders of finish was the same as their birth order.
2. Bonnie was born after Blair, Billy and Bert, but before Blake.
3. Bert was the oldest, and Billy was older than Blair.
4. Blake reached the top after Bonnie and Blair, but before Billy and the oldest child, who was last to the top.
5. Blair said "I'm tired" to Bonnie who was already on the top.
6. The last to the top said "never again," and the youngest said "whew."
7. Bonnie did not say "wow."

	Bonnie	Blake	Blair	Billy	Bert
1st born					
2nd born					
3rd born					
4th born					
5th born					
1st to top					
2nd to top					
3rd to top					
4th to top					
5th to top					
"I'm tired"					
"Whew"					
"Made it"					
"Wow"					
"Never again"					

 © 2005 MindWare

28 Rolling, Rolling, Rolling!

THE STORY

Five children named Mike, Mavis, Monica, Mark and Mary decided to race down Skull Mountain. They all used wheels, but everyone used something different. They raced using a skateboard, a wagon, a bicycle, a scooter and in-line skates. For the race, they all wore safety helmets of different colors; they were purple, green, orange, blue and yellow. When the race was over, the children had finished in 1st, 2nd, 3rd, 4th and 5th places. Based on the clues, match the children with what they raced with, the color of their helmets, and their order of finish.

THE CLUES

1. Monica finished ahead of Mike, Mavis, Mark and Mary.
2. Mary finished behind Mike, Mavis and Mark.
3. Mavis finished in front of Mike and Mark, and Mike finished behind Mark.
4. The first two finishers in the race rode a skateboard and a wagon and wore orange and yellow helmets.
5. The child in the green helmet, who rode a scooter, finished last.
6. Monica did not ride a wagon or wear a yellow helmet.
7. Mark did not ride a bicycle or wear a blue helmet.

	Mike	Mavis	Monica	Mark	Mary
Skateboard					
Wagon					
Bicycle					
Scooter					
Skates					
Purple helmet					
Green helmet					
Orange helmet					
Blue helmet					
Yellow helmet					
1st place					
2nd place					
3rd place					
4th place					
5th place					

© 2005 MindWare

29 Spaghetti and Meatballs

THE STORY

Fred, Frank, Farrah, Fran and Ferris were the five chef finalists in the National Spaghetti and Meatball Competition. The chefs were from Paris, London, New York, Berlin and Chicago. They used different kinds of meats for their meatballs. They used turkey, veal, pork, beef and chicken. They finished in 1st, 2nd, 3rd, 4th and 5th places. Based on the clues, match the chefs with their cities, the meats used in their meatballs, and their order of finish in the competition.

THE CLUES

1. Fran and Ferris did not use turkey, veal or pork meatballs with their spaghetti.
2. Frank placed after Farrah but ahead of Fred, Fran and Ferris and, of course, Fred placed in front of Fran, and Fran placed in front of Ferris.
3. The chefs from Berlin and Chicago used beef and chicken meatballs with their spaghetti.
4. The 3rd place chef from Paris used pork meatballs, and the 2nd place chef was not from London.
5. Fran did not use chicken meatballs because the Chicago chef used them.
6. The judges liked turkey meatballs with spaghetti the best.

	Fred	Frank	Farrah	Fran	Ferris
Paris					
London					
New York					
Berlin					
Chicago					
Turkey					
Veal					
Pork					
Beef					
Chicken					
1st place					
2nd place					
3rd place					
4th place					
5th place					

 © 2005 MindWare

30 Stewing Cats

THE STORY

Five cats named Tabitha, Tabby, Tammie, Teresa and Tillie all had secret family recipes for preparing mouse stew. Of course the recipes had much in common that we all associate with mouse stew, such as potatoes, carrots and rich gravy, but they all did have a unique ingredient. These ingredients were cheese, catnip, peanuts, basil and oregano. The cats served their stews with different kinds of bread. They served rye bread, French bread, pita bread, wheat bread and white bread. Each of the cats served a different beverage with their stew. They served root beer, iced tea, grape juice, ginger ale and lemonade. Based on the clues, match the cats with their secret ingredients, their types of bread and their beverages.

THE CLUES

1. Tabitha, Tabby and Tammie did not use either cheese or peanuts as secret ingredients, and none of them served wheat bread or white bread with their recipes.
2. Teresa and Tillie did not serve iced tea, ginger ale or lemonade.
3. Teresa tasted another cat's recipe that contained peanuts and was served with wheat bread and grape juice, and she thought it did not taste good.
4. Tammie did not like the taste of both basil and oregano, and she never served ginger ale or lemonade with her stew.
5. Iced tea was served with pita bread, and Tabby did not use basil or serve French bread or lemonade with her stew.

	Tabitha	Tabby	Tammie	Teresa	Tillie
Cheese					
Catnip					
Peanuts					
Basil					
Oregano					
Rye bread					
French bread					
Pita bread					
Wheat bread					
White bread					
Root beer					
Iced tea					
Grape juice					
Ginger ale					
Lemonade					

© 2005 MindWare

31 Family Confusion

THE STORY

Five sisters from the same family named Bess, Betty, Belinda, Bonnie and Barb were married to Bob Smith, Ben Doe, Byron Wu, Bill Jones and Bart Villars. Each of the married couples had two children. Each couple had one son and one daughter. The boys were named Bob, Ben, Byron, Bill and Bart, but no son had the same first name as his father. The girls were named Bess, Betty, Belinda, Bonnie and Barb, but no daughter had the same first name as her mother. Based on the clues, match the mother's first name with their husband's full name, and the names of their sons and daughters.

THE CLUES

1. No children had the same first name as their mothers or fathers.
2. Bess, Betty and Belinda were not married to either Bob Smith or Ben Doe.
3. Barb was not Mrs. Doe, Bess had the shortest married name, and Belinda was not Mrs. Jones.
4. Bess' son was named after his uncle Mr. Jones, and Bonnie's son was named after Bess' husband.
5. Barb's son was named after his uncle, who was married to his Aunt Bonnie.
6. Neither Bill nor Bart had sisters named Belinda, Bonnie or Barb.
7. Bob's sister was named in honor of his Aunt Smith.

	Bess	Betty	Belinda	Bonnie	Barb
Bob Smith					
Ben Doe					
Byron Wu					
Bill Jones					
Bart Villars					
Bob					
Ben					
Byron					
Bill					
Bart					
Bess					
Betty					
Belinda					
Bonnie					
Barb					

 © 2005 MindWare

32 Halloween Fun

THE STORY

Five animals named Peggy, Pauline, Patrick, Pierre and Phillip lived together on the Brown Farm and decided to have a Halloween party. They were a goat, a pig, a cow, a horse and a donkey. For their Halloween costumes, they dressed as a pirate, a princess, a pumpkin, a jockey and a ballerina. They all brought their favorite candy to the party. These candies were jellybeans, licorice, gumdrops, chocolate and marshmallows. Based on the clues, match the animal names with their types, their costumes and their favorite candies.

THE CLUES

1. Peggy thought the cow in the princess costume should have worn a larger size.
2. Pauline thought the horse in the jockey costume was making the wrong statement.
3. Patrick thought the pig in the ballerina costume, that loved jellybeans, looked beautiful.
4. Pierre thought the licorice-loving donkey in the pirate costume looked quite dashing.
5. Phillip thought the marshmallow-loving goat in the pumpkin costume could have been more creative.
6. Patrick, Pierre and Phillip were not cows.
7. Peggy did not dress as a jockey or a ballerina, and Pauline did not like gumdrops.
8. Patrick was not a goat or a donkey.
9. Pierre was not a goat.

	Peggy	Pauline	Patrick	Pierre	Phillip
Goat					
Pig					
Cow					
Horse					
Donkey					
Pirate					
Princess					
Pumpkin					
Jockey					
Ballerina					
Jellybeans					
Licorice					
Gumdrops					
Chocolate					
Marshmallows					

© 2005 MindWare

33 Fishing Around

THE STORY

Sidney, Sara, Sal, Sammi and Shawn went fishing together. They all went casting for fish, and by the end of the day, they had all made a different number of casts. These casting amounts were 500 casts, 750 casts, 1000 casts, 1500 casts and 1657 casts. They all caught only one fish apiece. They caught a bass, a trout, a perch, a pike and a carp. The fish weighed different amounts. They weighed 1 pound, 2 pounds, 3 pounds, 5 pounds and 6 pounds. Based on the clues, match the fishermen with the number of casts, the type of fish they caught and the weights of the fish.

THE CLUES

1. Sidney, Sara and Sal made the most casts but they ended up with the lightest fish.
2. Sidney and Sammi caught the pike and the carp.
3. Sal cast twice as much as Sammi but less than Sidney, who cast twice as much as Shawn.
4. Sidney's fish weighed twice as much as Sara's perch.
5. The second heaviest fish was a pike, and the heaviest fish was a trout.

	Sidney	Sara	Sal	Sammi	Shawn
500 casts					
750 casts					
1000 casts					
1500 casts					
1657 casts					
Bass					
Trout					
Perch					
Pike					
Carp					
1 pound					
2 pounds					
3 pounds					
5 pounds					
6 pounds					

 © 2005 MindWare

34 Dinner for Five

THE STORY

James, Jane, Jake, Janet and Joe went out for something to eat at a small diner. The diner only had five seats and the seats were numbered 1, 2, 3, 4 and 5. They ordered different sandwiches that were filled with ham, cheese, bologna, salami and bacon. They ordered different beverages. They ordered tea, coffee, milk, cola and water. When the waiter brought the orders, he managed to get everything mixed up and nobody was correctly served the sandwich or beverage that they had ordered. Based on the clues, match the names with their seat numbers, the sandwiches they ordered and the beverages they ordered.

THE CLUES

1. Nobody was served what he or she ordered.
2. James was served a salami sandwich with tea, Jane was served a bacon sandwich with milk, Jake was served a ham sandwich with coffee, and Janet was served a bologna sandwich with water.
3. Jane's seat number was twice as big as James' seat number, but her seat number was only half as big as Janet's seat number.
4. Jake's seat number was larger than Joe's seat number.
5. Jake, Janet and Joe ordered ham, cheese and bologna.
6. The person in seat 4 ordered a cheese sandwich and cola.
7. Joe did not order tea, coffee or milk.
8. Jake did not order milk.

	James	Jane	Jake	Janet	Joe
Seat 1					
Seat 2					
Seat 3					
Seat 4					
Seat 5					
Ham					
Cheese					
Bologna					
Salami					
Bacon					
Tea					
Coffee					
Milk					
Cola					
Water					

35 Fair Enough

THE STORY

Five friends named Elsbeth, Eliot, Erin, Eddie and Edith entered three contests at the Kenosha County Fair. The first contest was the pie-eating contest. They ate 10 pies, 15 pies, 20 pies, 30 pies and 37 pies. The second contest they entered was the sack race. They finished in 1st place, 2nd place, 3rd place, 4th place and 5th place. The third contest they entered was a corn-shucking contest. In one minute, they shucked 10 ears, 15 ears, 20 ears, 30 ears and 37 ears. Based on the clues, match the friends with the number of pies they ate, their order of finish in the sack race, and the number of ears of corn they shucked.

THE CLUES

1. No one matched their pie eating totals with their corn shucking totals.
2. Erin ate twice as many pies as Elsbeth and five more pies than Eliot, but Eddie ate twice as many pies as Eliot.
3. In the sack race, Edith did the best, Erin did the worst, and Elsbeth did worse than Eliot but better than Eddie.
4. Edith shucked twice as many ears of corn as Elsbeth.
5. Eliot shucked twice as many ears of corn as Erin.

	Elsbeth	Eliot	Erin	Eddie	Edith
10 pies					
15 pies					
20 pies					
30 pies					
37 pies					
1st place					
2nd place					
3rd place					
4th place					
5th place					
10 ears					
15 ears					
20 ears					
30 ears					
37 ears					

 © 2005 MindWare

36 Frog Frolics

THE STORY

Five frogs named Frank, Farrah, Faith, Fred and Phillip held three contests to see which frog was the best at doing what frogs do best. The first contest was a fly eating contest. In one minute they ate 5 flies, 10 flies, 15 flies, 22 flies and 30 flies. The second contest was a hopping contest. The frogs hopped 5 feet, 10 feet, 15 feet, 22 feet and 30 feet. The third contest was to see which frog could croak the most times in a minute. They croaked 5 croaks, 10 croaks, 15 croaks, 22 croaks and 30 croaks. Based on the clues, match the frogs with their fly eating totals, their hopping totals and their croaking totals.

THE CLUES

1. No frogs' total number in any contest was matched by the same number in any other activity.
2. Phillip ate twice as many flies as Faith, but did not eat the most flies.
3. Fred ate more flies than Frank, but fewer than Farrah.
4. Farrah hopped twice as far as Fred, and Frank hopped twice as far as Faith.
5. Phillip did not croak the most or the least.
6. Fred did not croak the most, and Frank did not croak the least.

	Frank	Farrah	Faith	Fred	Phillip
5 flies					
10 flies					
15 flies					
22 flies					
30 flies					
5 feet					
10 feet					
15 feet					
22 feet					
30 feet					
5 croaks					
10 croaks					
15 croaks					
22 croaks					
30 croaks					

37 School Science Fair

THE STORY

Five students named Deke, Dave, Diane, Daphne and Dale won the top five places in the Lavender Hill Elementary School's annual science fair. Their teachers were Mr. Porter, Mr. Butler, Mrs. Skinner, Ms. Spencer and Mrs. Blake. The students won 1st, 2nd, 3rd, 4th and 5th places. Their science projects had something to do with string, pulleys, magnets, a volcano and a doorbell. Based on the clues, match the students with their teachers, their order of finish, and their award winning science fair projects.

THE CLUES

1. Mr. Butler's student with the science project that dealt with string, finished after Mr. Porter's student, but Ms. Spencer's student with the homemade volcano won first place.
2. The male teachers were proud of their students who did something with string and pulleys, but Mrs. Skinner's student, who used magnets, won third place.
3. Dave, Diane and Daphne did not finish first or last.
4. The second place student's science fair project was a doorbell.
5. Deke did not finish in first place, Diane finished after Daphne, and Dave finished after Diane.

	Deke	Dave	Diane	Daphne	Dale
Mr. Porter					
Mr. Butler					
Mrs. Skinner					
Ms. Spencer					
Mrs. Blake					
1st place					
2nd place					
3rd place					
4th place					
5th place					
String					
Pulleys					
Magnets					
Volcano					
Doorbell					

 © 2005 MindWare

38 Did You Drop That?

THE STORY

Hank, Harriet, Harold, Hester and Hiram, whose last names were Dixie, Pinkney, Smedley, Putney and Snider all bought classic cars last month. They bought a Packard, Desoto, Edsel, Nash and Hudson. Unfortunately, as they were driving their cars home, something fell off all of them with a loud clang. The things that fell off were a sprocket, a widget, a whatsis, a thingie and a whosit. The cars were different colors and were green, yellow, orange, pink and red. Based on the clues, match the first and last names, the names of the cars, the things that fell off of them and their colors.

THE CLUES

1. Snider bought the green Packard that lost its thingie.
2. The Nash was pink and did not lose a sprocket because it was Pinkney's red Hudson that lost a sprocket.
3. Harriet was not named Dixie, and she did not buy a red car.
4. Hank, Harriet and Hester were not named Putney or Snider.
5. The Packard and Desoto lost a thingie and a whosit, but maybe not in that order.
6. Putney did not drive a Packard or a Desoto, and his car was orange and lost a whatsis.
7. Hank, Harriet and Harold did not drive a Packard or a Desoto.
8. The Edsel, Nash and Hudson were orange, pink and red, but maybe not in that order.

	Hank	Harriet	Harold	Hester	Hiram
Dixie					
Pinkney					
Smedley					
Putney					
Snider					
Packard					
Desoto					
Edsel					
Nash					
Hudson					
Sprocket					
Widget					
Whatsis					
Thingie					
Whosit					
Green					
Yellow					
Orange					
Pink					
Red					

© 2005 MindWare

39 Catfish Complaints

THE STORY

Five catfish named Whiskers, Tabby, Tom, Bubbles and Fred were sitting around the bottom of their pond discussing various subjects. They discussed their favorite foods, which were frogs, worms, cheese balls, snails and crawdads. The catfish were generally good-natured but they all had one thing they really disliked. They disliked fishermen, carp, minnows, bass and eels. The catfish weighed 4, 5, 8, 15 and 16 pounds. They all had their favorite months of the year, which were March, June, July, October and December. Based on the clues, match the catfish with their favorite foods, the things they disliked, their weights and their favorite months.

THE CLUES

1. Tabby's favorite month came before Bubble's favorite month and after the month preferred by Whiskers.
2. The lightest catfish's favorite month was the earliest month shown, and the heaviest catfish loved December.
3. Tabby, Tom and Bubbles thought fishermen and carp were not so bad.
4. Fred weighed twice as much as Tabby, and Tabby weighed twice as much as Tom, but Bubbles weighed more than Tabby.
5. The heaviest catfish ate cheese balls, the lightest catfish ate crawdads, and the lightest catfish did not dislike minnows or eels because he thought they were cute.
6. Tabby never ate snails or frogs, and it was the catfish that disliked carp that ate frogs.
7. The snail-eating catfish disliked eels because he thought they were creepy looking.

	Whiskers	Tabby	Tom	Bubbles	Fred
Frogs					
Worms					
Cheese balls					
Snails					
Crawdads					
Fishermen					
Carp					
Minnows					
Bass					
Eels					
4 pounds					
5 pounds					
8 pounds					
15 pounds					
16 pounds					
March					
June					
July					
October					
December					

 © 2005 MindWare

40 Everything's Relative

THE STORY

Five men named Max, Mark, Mike, Mickey and Martin were good friends. They each had one son and one daughter. Their sons were named George, Greg, Gale, Gunther and Godfrey. Their daughters were named Georgina, Gail, Greta, Gertrude and Gina. Much to their delight, the five sons married the five daughters but, of course, no brothers and sisters married each other. This puzzle has two parts. In the first part, you must identify each man with his son and daughter. In the second part, using information from the first part and the clues, you must figure out which sons and daughters make up each of the five couples.

THE CLUES

1. Mickey and Martin did not have sons named Greg, Gunther and Godfrey, or daughters named Georgina, Gail and Gina.
2. Mickey's daughter was not Gertrude, but Gertrude's brother was George.
3. Gunther's sister was Georgina, and Gina's brother was Greg and, of course, Mark's son was not Godfrey because Godfrey's sister was Gail.
4. Max's son was not Greg or Gunther, and Mike's daughter was not Gina.
5. Couples 1, 2 and 3 did not include Greg, Gunther, Gail or Gina.
6. Mark's daughter-in-law is Gail who is not a part of couple 5, and Mike's son-in-law is not a part of couple 4.
7. Couple 3 consists of a boy whose brother-in-law is George and, of course, that is not Gail's brother.
8. Couple 1 consists of Gale's brother-in-law and Gertrude's sister-in-law.

	Max	Mark	Mike	Mickey	Martin
George					
Greg					
Gale					
Gunther					
Godfrey					
Georgina					
Gail					
Greta					
Gertrude					
Gina					

	1st Couple	2nd Couple	3rd Couple	4th Couple	5th Couple
George					
Greg					
Gale					
Gunther					
Godfrey					
Georgina					
Gail					
Greta					
Gertrude					
Gina					

© 2005 MindWare

41 Warthogs Cook

THE STORY

The top five finishers in the annual warthog cooking contest were Wanda, Wendy, Winnie, Wilma and Winona. Their last names were Stockley, Spreckley, Slader, Portal and Snead. They finished in 1st, 2nd, 3rd, 4th and 5th places. For the competition they wore aprons that were red, yellow, black, blue and green. Naturally, they spent some time getting their food entries just right. The time spent was 2, 3, 4, 6 and 7 hours. Based on the clues, match the first names with their last names, their finishing places, the color of their aprons, and the number of hours spent on their food entries.

THE CLUES

1. Spreckley, in the blue apron, spent 7 hours on her food entry and yet managed only to finish ahead of one other warthog cooking contestant.
2. Wanda spent twice as much time on her food entry as Wendy, while Winnie spent half as much time on her entry as Wilma.
3. Stockley and Spreckley finished in the last two places even though they spent the most time on their food entries.
4. Wanda did not wear green, and Snead wore the red apron and finished in front of the warthog in the green apron.
5. Wanda, Wendy and Winnie took the top three places, but maybe not in that order.
6. Wendy thought green made Slader look taller, but she thought Portal looked tired in her black apron, and she could not believe that Portal won the competition!

	Wanda	Wendy	Winnie	Wilma	Winona
Stockley					
Spreckley					
Slader					
Portal					
Snead					
1st place					
2nd place					
3rd place					
4th place					
5th place					
Red apron					
Yellow apron					
Black apron					
Blue apron					
Green apron					
2 hours					
3 hours					
4 hours					
6 hours					
7 hours					

 | © 2005 MindWare

42 Movie Magic

THE STORY

Five movie directors named Roman, Roland, Roger, Richard and Raymond, whose last names were Wooley, Webber, Wolsey, Weeley and Wacker, directed movies in five different cities. The cities were Chicago, New York, Miami, Seattle and Boston. The names of the movies were Deeptanic, Sinktanic, Yawntanic, Dozetanic and Wetanic. The movies were released in different months of the same year. They were released in January, March, May, June and October. Based on the clues, match the first names with the last names, the cities where the movies were shot, the names of the movies, and the months when they were released.

THE CLUES

1. The movie filmed in Seattle was not Deeptanic and was released first but, of course, Dozetanic was released after Sinktanic and Deeptanic and before Wetanic, which was released last.
2. Yawntanic, filmed in Boston, was released after Sinktanic and Deeptanic were released but before the movies made in New York and Chicago were released.
3. Wolsey and Webber did not film in Boston, and Webber did not film in Seattle either.
4. Raymond was not Webber, and Roman was not Weeley because Weeley filmed in Miami.
5. Roman, a man of strong opinions, thought Webber was not very talented, Richard was egotistical, and Wacker was foolish for filming Wetanic in Chicago.
6. Roland did not film in Chicago, and his last name was not Webber, Wooley or Weeley.

	Roman	Roland	Roger	Richard	Raymond
Wooley					
Webber					
Wolsey					
Weeley					
Wacker					
Chicago					
New York					
Miami					
Seattle					
Boston					
Deeptanic					
Sinktanic					
Yawntanic					
Dozetanic					
Wetanic					
January					
March					
May					
June					
October					

© 2005 MindWare

43 Did I Order That?

THE STORY

Elvira, Edward, Ernie, Ellie and Ernst went out together for a meal. The main dishes they ordered were steak, chicken, shrimp, lobster and perch. The side dishes they ordered were potatoes, spinach, beans, corn and beets. For dessert, they ordered pie, cake, pudding, ice cream and a tart. Their beverages were coffee, cola, tea, lemonade and milk. Their waitress, Inez, managed to mix-up the orders so completely that none of the five diners got anything that they ordered delivered to them correctly. Based on the clues, see if you can figure out exactly what each person actually ordered.

THE CLUES

1. Elvira was incorrectly served steak, potatoes, cake and coffee.
2. Edward was incorrectly served chicken, spinach, pie and cola.
3. Ernie was incorrectly served shrimp, beans, ice cream and milk.
4. Ellie was incorrectly served lobster, corn, a tart and lemonade.
5. Elvira gave the main dish she was served to Ernie, and Ernie gave his to Edward.
6. Ellie is allergic to seafood, and Elvira does not eat lobster.
7. The three who ordered seafood also ordered potatoes, spinach, corn, pie, cake, a tart, coffee, lemonade and milk.
8. Elvira gave her potatoes to the person who ordered lobster, and the person who ordered lobster did not order pie, cake, lemonade or milk.
9. Ellie exchanged drinks with Edward.

	Elvira	Edward	Ernie	Ellie	Ernst
Steak					
Chicken					
Shrimp					
Lobster					
Perch					
Potatoes					
Spinach					
Beans					
Corn					
Beets					
Pie					
Cake					
Pudding					
Ice cream					
Tart					
Coffee					
Cola					
Tea					
Lemonade					
Milk					

 © 2005 MindWare

44 Band of Gorillas

THE STORY

Five gorillas named Gordon, Gayle, George, Gregory and Ginny were all musically talented and played two musical instruments. They all played different types of horns. They played a tuba, a trumpet, a trombone, a saxophone and a bugle. They also played different stringed instruments. The stringed instruments were a banjo, a guitar, a violin, a cello and a harp. They wanted to form a band but could not agree on a name for the band. Each gorilla had a band name they wanted to adopt. These band names were The Whew, Spice Gorillas, Milli Gorilli, Apeful Dead and 5 Ape Night. While they were arguing about band names, they ate bananas. They ate 14 bananas, 28 bananas, 30 bananas, 60 bananas and 61 bananas. Based on the clues, match the gorillas with the horns they played, the stringed instruments they played, their favored band name, and the number of bananas they ate.

THE CLUES

1. Gordon ate half as many bananas as Gregory, and Gayle ate twice as many bananas as Ginny but, of course, Gordon ate more bananas than Ginny.
2. Gordon and Gayle played the saxophone, bugle, banjo and guitar, and did not like the names Apeful Dead or 5 Ape Night.
3. George did not play the trumpet, trombone, cello or harp.
4. The trumpet-playing gorilla played the cello and favored the name 5 Ape Night.
5. Ginny did not play the cello or tuba, and George did not like the Apeful Dead name.
6. A gorilla that ate twice as many bananas as another gorilla played the saxophone and banjo.
7. Gayle did not care for the names The Whew and Milli Gorilli.
8. Gordon did not care for the name The Whew.

	Gordon	Gayle	George	Gregory	Ginny
Tuba					
Trumpet					
Trombone					
Saxophone					
Bugle					
Banjo					
Guitar					
Violin					
Cello					
Harp					
The Whew					
Spice Gorillas					
Milli Gorilli					
Apeful Dead					
5 Ape Night					
14 bananas					
28 bananas					
30 bananas					
60 bananas					
61 bananas					

45 A New Show

THE STORY

Tom, Tess, Tillie, Toula and Terry worked for a television network as writers. They were assigned to work together to create five new characters for a new children's program. Each of the writers came up with different cute characters that were named Kiki, Kaka, Koko, Kuku and Keke. The new characters were blue, green, pink, orange and purple. On the show, the characters rode a bicycle, a skateboard, a unicycle, a tricycle and a scooter. Each of the characters was assigned a special word that only that character would say. These special words were "boing," "booboo," "bummer," "bink" and "babaloo." Based on the clues, match the writers with the new characters, their colors, what they rode and their special words.

THE CLUES

1. Toula and Terry created Kaka and Koko who were not blue, green or pink, but they did ride a unicycle and a tricycle and said "bink" and "babaloo."
2. The orange character rode a unicycle, the green character said "booboo" all the time, and the pink character rode a bicycle.
3. Toula's character was not orange and it did not say "bink."
4. Tom thought Tess' character would have looked better riding a skateboard in either blue or pink, but those colors were already taken.
5. Tillie's character was not pink, Kiki was blue but did not say "bummer."
6. Tess did not create Keke, and Koko said "bink."

	Tom	Tess	Tillie	Toula	Terry
Kiki					
Kaka					
Koko					
Kuku					
Keke					
Blue					
Green					
Pink					
Orange					
Purple					
Bicycle					
Skateboard					
Unicycle					
Tricycle					
Scooter					
"Boing"					
"Booboo"					
"Bummer"					
"Bink"					
"Babaloo"					

 © 2005 MindWare

46 It's News To Me!

THE STORY

Five newspaper reporters named Biff, Betsy, Bonnie, Byron and Bill found themselves stranded together at an airport. Their last names were Lincoln, Grant, Hayes, Tilden and Wilson. They lived in different cities. The cities were New York, Chicago, Boston, Seattle and San Diego. The newspapers they worked for were The Post, The Tribune, The Dispatch, The Times and The Globe. The areas of news they covered were crime, politics, finance, sports and entertainment. Based on the clues, match the first names with their last names, their cities, their newspapers, and the news areas they wrote about.

THE CLUES

1. The finance writer lived in Seattle, worked for The Post, and did not have the name Lincoln or Grant.
2. The sports writer lived in San Diego, worked for The Globe, and did not have the name Lincoln or Grant.
3. The entertainment writer lived in New York, wrote for The Times, and did not have the name Lincoln or Grant.
4. Biff and Betsy were not named Hayes, Tilden or Wilson.
5. Bonnie and Byron were not finance reporters.
6. Bonnie did not live in San Diego, but had visited Wilson's home there.
7. Bonnie was not Tilden, Betsy was not the Boston politics writer.
8. The Dispatch did not have a crime writer or a writer named Lincoln.

	Biff	Betsy	Bonnie	Byron	Bill
Lincoln					
Grant					
Hayes					
Tilden					
Wilson					
New York					
Chicago					
Boston					
Seattle					
San Diego					
The Post					
The Tribune					
The Dispatch					
The Times					
The Globe					
Crime					
Politics					
Finance					
Sports					
Entertainment					

© 2005 MindWare

47 Educational Theory

THE STORY

Tom was surprised when he received his class schedule for the new school year. Instead of going to five different classes every day, he would be having one subject all day for each day of the week. One day a week, he would be taking English, math, history, geography or logic. The teachers for these subjects were Mr. Nixon, Mr. Carter, Mrs. Johnson, Mrs. Reagan and Mrs. Truman. They taught in rooms 300, 301, 302, 304 and 306. No matter what outfits they wore, the teachers always wore the same color shoes. These favored shoe colors were black, brown, blue, red and yellow. Based on the clues, figure out Tom's schedule; match the days of the week with the subjects, the teachers, the room numbers and the teacher's shoe colors.

THE CLUES

1. Tom lost his schedule and went to school early looking for help. He met a teacher in blue shoes who looked at a computer and said, "Do not bother to write this down. Since today is Monday, you will have history the day after tomorrow, my class the day after that, geography the day after that, and English the day after today."
2. The teacher continued, "Of course, this means that you will have Mrs. Johnson and Mrs. Truman at the end of the week, Mr. Nixon and Mr. Carter at the beginning of the week, and Mrs. Reagan in the middle of the week, and you have already met the logic teacher despite the fact that all five teachers are new and my name is not Mrs. Truman."
3. The teacher went on, "You will report to Mr. Nixon tomorrow, to Mrs. Truman in Room 300, I have the highest room number, the history teacher has the second highest room number, and the math room is not 301."
4. Finally, the teacher said, "For your information, the English teacher always wears yellow shoes, the geography teacher always wears red shoes, and the history teacher never wears black shoes."

	Monday	Tuesday	Wednesday	Thursday	Friday
English					
Math					
History					
Geography					
Logic					
Mr. Nixon					
Mr. Carter					
Mrs. Johnson					
Mrs. Reagan					
Mrs. Truman					
Room 300					
Room 301					
Room 302					
Room 304					
Room 306					
Black shoes					
Brown shoes					
Blue shoes					
Red shoes					
Yellow shoes					

 © 2005 MindWare

48 Early Achievements

THE STORY

Scientists recently discovered records of five Stone Age inventors named Ooga, Egga, Ugga, Aaga and Iggy. They belonged to different tribes: the Whosees, the Whatsees, the Wheresees, the Whensees and the Whysees. Their early inventions were cooking, washing, underwear, shoes and a stone axe. The tribes sought shelter in various ways and lived in caves, in trees, in huts, in holes and under rocks. The tribes painted themselves different colors. These tribal colors were blue, pink, orange, red and yellow. Based on the clues, match the Stone Age inventors with their tribes, their inventions, their tribal shelters and their tribal colors.

THE CLUES

1. The Whosees were the first people in history to eat cooked food, though their custom of living in trees and painting themselves orange never caught on.
2. The Whensees were the first people to think of washing themselves, but living in caves and painting oneself yellow has declined in recent years.
3. Aaga and Iggy were not Whosees or Whensees, and Ooga always ate raw food and never washed.
4. Ugga was able to find a husband despite the fact she never washed.
5. Iggy did not invent shoes or a stone axe.
6. You cannot wear Aaga's invention, Aaga did not live in a hut or under rocks, and Aaga was never painted pink or red.
7. The Whatsees lived in holes and painted themselves blue.
8. A Wheresee invented underwear, and the Whysees lived in huts and painted themselves red.

	Ooga	Egga	Ugga	Aaga	Iggy
Whosees					
Whatsees					
Wheresees					
Whensees					
Whysees					
Cooking					
Washing					
Underwear					
Shoes					
Stone axe					
Caves					
Trees					
Huts					
Holes					
Under rocks					
Blue					
Pink					
Orange					
Red					
Yellow					

© 2005 MindWare

49 Sun Safety

THE STORY

Five young ladies named Jill, Jane, Joan, Jenny and Joanna were lucky winners of free trips to five different holiday locations. They won trips to Mexico, Florida, Bermuda, Spain and Aruba. In preparation for their trips, they all went out and purchased five different brands of sunscreen. These brands were TanEz, TanOk, TanBest, TanSafe and Tanique. They paid $2, $3, $4, $5 and $10. The sunscreens all had different sun protection factors. These were factor 5, factor 10, factor 30, factor 35 and factor 40. Based on the clues, match the young ladies with their holiday destinations, the names of the sunscreen they purchased, the cost of their sunscreens and their sunscreen factors.

THE CLUES

1. Jill and Jane were not going to Mexico, Florida or Bermuda, neither Joan nor Jenny was going to Florida, and Joan was not going to Bermuda.
2. Jill spent twice as much as Jenny but less than Joan, who spent half as much as Joanna.
3. The most expensive brand was TanSafe and the least expensive brand was Tanique.
4. Jane's TanOk cost more than Jenny's sunscreen, but was $2 less than TanEz.
5. The cheapest sunscreen had the lowest factor, and the highest factor was half the price of another sunscreen.
6. The girl traveling to Spain purchased factor 30 and paid twice as much for it as the girl who purchased factor 5.
7. Factor 35 sunscreen cost more than factor 10 sunscreen.

	Jill	Jane	Joan	Jenny	Joanna
Mexico					
Florida					
Bermuda					
Spain					
Aruba					
TanEz					
TanOk					
TanBest					
TanSafe					
Tanique					
$2					
$3					
$4					
$5					
$10					
Factor 5					
Factor 10					
Factor 30					
Factor 35					
Factor 40					

 © 2005 MindWare

50 Farm Errands

THE STORY

Five farmers named Bert, Betty, Belle, Brad and Ben whose last names were Polk, Adams, Tyler, Taylor and Grant went to town one recent day. They all brought produce to sell at the market. They brought potatoes, tomatoes, corn, beans and squash. They also all had other reasons to come to town. These reasons were to get a haircut, to go to the dentist, to buy seed, to buy fertilizer, and to visit a sick friend. While in town, they all purchased a different animal to take back to the farm. They purchased a duck, a goose, a goat, a pig and a cow. Based on the clues, match the first names with the last names, the produce they sold, the other reasons for them to come to town and the animals they purchased.

THE CLUES

1. Belle, Brad and Ben were not named Polk or Adams and they did not grow either potatoes or tomatoes.
2. Bert and Betty did not go to town for seed, fertilizer, or to visit a sick friend.
3. Brad and Ben purchased birds in town.
4. Adams grew tomatoes, got a haircut, and purchased a cow.
5. Grant grew beans, visited a sick friend, and purchased a goat.
6. Betty did not buy a pig, and Brad did not grow squash.
7. Tyler grew squash, and Taylor purchased fertilizer and a goose.

	Bert	Betty	Belle	Brad	Ben
Polk					
Adams					
Tyler					
Taylor					
Grant					
Potatoes					
Tomatoes					
Corn					
Beans					
Squash					
Haircut					
Dentist					
Seed					
Fertilizer					
Sick friend					
Duck					
Goose					
Goat					
Pig					
Cow					

© 2005 MindWare

Answers

1. Is Three Enough?

Bess	Betty	Bertha
John	Joe	Jerry
Fireman	Barber	Lawyer
Bill	Bart	Bob
Sarah	Sheila	Shana

2. Playing Chicken

Henny	Penny	Jenny
Goose	Crow	Duck
Mary	Mattie	Millie
Watching TV	Playing cards	Telling stories
Poetry	Egg raising	Cooking

3. Pond Life

Frank	Fran	Fred
Carp	Catfish	Bass
4 pounds	5 pounds	2 pounds
Crawfish	Minnows	Tadpoles
Green	Orange	Red

4. The Bike Ride

Walter	Wilma	Warren
Orange bike	Red bike	Black bike
Red shirt	Black shirt	Orange shirt
Hot dog	Taco	Hamburger
Lemonade	Root beer	Iced tea

5. Fun in the Park

Ken	Keith	Kathy	Kate
Bread	Bologna	Mustard	Lemonade
Yellow shoes	Purple shoes	Pink shoes	White shoes
Bee	Yellow jacket	Hornet	Wasp
"Mommy"	"Drat"	"Jeepers"	"Yowzer"

6. Breakfast Food

Victor	Val	Virginia	Vinnie
Stanley Cup	Tea Cup	Coffee Cup	Cozy Cup
Cheese	Onion	Bacon	Ham
Waffles	Pancakes	French toast	Crepes
Tomato juice	Milk	Coffee	Tea

7. Sinking Ships

Captain Hoover	Captain Adams	Captain Ford	Captain Johnson
Sea Witch	Sea Otter	Sea Belle	Sea Sprite
Tornado	Blizzard	Typhoon	Hurricane
30 sailors	25 sailors	10 sailors	20 sailors
25 days	30 days	20 days	10 days

8. Yachts of Luck

Zeke	Zelda	Zoe	Zach
Ripper	Speedy	Flyer	Demon
15 miles	13 miles	12 miles	6 miles
Broken mast	Broken rudder	Sprung a leak	Hit a rock
$21,000	$22,000	$20,000	$10,000

9. Don't Buy It

Edith	Elmo	Eddie	Ellen
Don's Auctions	Cal's Auctions	Al's Auctions	Bea's Auctions
Painting	Desk	Bed warmer	Chair
Duke	Earl	Prince	Dame
$62	$25	$50	$64

10. Executives

Joan	Jim	Josh	Jean
Accounting	Production	Sales	Shipping
150 employees	100 employees	200 employees	300 employees
39 years old	34 years old	30 years old	60 years old
6 gold watches	3 gold watches	9 gold watches	12 gold watches

11. First Ladies

Connie	Cathy	Carol	Callie
Farley	Fowler	Frye	Fuller
First baby	First marriage	First job	First birthday
Black eyes	Brown eyes	Blue eyes	Green eyes
Brown hair	Black hair	Green hair	Blue hair

12. Late for School

Dan	Diana	Donna	Del
Adams	Jefferson	Monroe	Madison
Tuesday	Thursday	Friday	Monday
8th grade	7th grade	5th grade	6th grade
Power outage	Overslept	Missed bus	Forgot

13. Frog Kissing Perils

Will	Walt	Warren	Winston	Weston
8 frogs	16 frogs	12 frogs	24 frogs	22 frogs
Helga	Helveta	Hortense	Harriet	Hilda
Gopher	Vole	Goat	Skink	Newt

14. Walking Robins

Frank	Farah	Fran	Farley	Frieda
Chicago	Toledo	New York	Detroit	Albany
8 miles	4 miles	2 miles	5 miles	6 miles
Tijuana	Tampico	Acapulco	Mexicali	Oaxaca

15. Fast Food Logic

Greg	Gail	Gaylord	Gina	George
4th in line	3rd in line	5th in line	2nd in line	1st in line
Gyro	Burger	Hot dog	Taco	Bratwurst
Lemonade	Tea	Coffee	Cola	Milk

16. June Birthdays

Edward	Ellie	Eilene	Ennis	Elsbeth
Fritz	Flynn	Freese	Funk	Fisher
June 10th	June 8th	June 9th	June 7th	June 6th
20 years old	40 years old	10 years old	15 years old	30 years old

 © 2005 MindWare

17. Fastest Pecking Awards

Becky	Billy	Bobby	Benny	Betsy
Duck	Goose	Turkey	Pigeon	Chicken
100 pecks	80 pecks	60 pecks	40 pecks	150 pecks
Neck strain	Crossed-eyes	Headache	Ringing ears	Bent beak

18. School Awards

Kate	Ken	Karen	Kyle	Knute
Kempe	Knoll	Knapper	Kersey	Kelly
Math	French	Science	English	Logic
97%	96%	100%	99%	98%

19. Basketball Team Logic

Norm	Nate	Neil	Nigel	Niles
Napton	Nabors	Nesbitt	Nielsen	Nolan
#10	#15	#20	#5	#7
10 points	15 points	20 points	7 points	5 points

20. Tearful Movie

Billy	Bob	Bert	Brenda	Barb
Driscoll	Dray	Driver	Durley	Drew
12 times	18 times	24 times	36 times	72 times
24 gallons	9 gallons	12 gallons	20 gallons	6 gallons

21. Mexican Food Mix-Up

Monday	Tuesday	Wednesday	Thursday	Friday
Tamales	Tostadas	Burritos	Tacos	Enchiladas
Beans	Rice	Nachos	Salad	Potatoes
Iced tea	Coffee	Cola	Root beer	Lemonade

22. School Organization

Alice	Bert	Carol	David	Elwood
Smythe	Smith	Schmit	Schultz	Smolt
Room 105	Room 102	Room 103	Room 104	Room 106
2nd grade	6th grade	3rd grade	4th grade	5th grade

23. Picnic in the Park

Helga	Henry	Helen	Harvey	Harold
Bread	Hot dogs	Pickles	Apples	Donuts
Root beer	Fruit punch	Iced tea	Lemonade	Cola
Blue bike	Green bike	Pink bike	Red bike	White bike

24. Howl Do You Like It?

Jack	Jane	Judy	Jill	Jimmy
40 seconds	45 seconds	30 seconds	20 seconds	60 seconds
Mice	Birds	Squirrels	Cats	Cars
Poodle	Beagle	Terrier	Elkhound	Collie

25. Baseball Players

Clara	Charles	Cathy	Cindi	Clark
3rd base	2nd base	1st base	Left field	Right field
#3	#4	#2	#18	#9
Lemon	Strawberry	Chocolate	Vanilla	Banana

26. Logical Lunch

Monday	Tuesday	Wednesday	Thursday	Friday
Fish	Meat loaf	Ham	Pot roast	Hamburger
Beets	Spinach	Potatoes	Carrots	Cabbage
Lemonade	Tea	Coffee	Milk	Cola

27. Mountain Climbing

Bonnie	Blake	Blair	Billy	Bert
4th born	5th born	3rd born	2nd born	1st born
1st to top	3rd to top	2nd to top	4th to top	5th to top
"Made it"	"Whew"	"I'm tired"	"Wow"	"Never again"

28. Rolling, Rolling, Rolling!

Mike	Mavis	Monica	Mark	Mary
Bicycle	Wagon	Skateboard	Skates	Scooter
Blue helmet	Yellow helmet	Orange helmet	Purple helmet	Green helmet
4th place	2nd place	1st place	3rd place	5th place

29. Spaghetti and Meatballs

Fred	Frank	Farrah	Fran	Ferris
Paris	New York	London	Berlin	Chicago
Pork	Veal	Turkey	Beef	Chicken
3rd place	2nd place	1st place	4th place	5th place

30. Stewing Cats

Tabitha	Tabby	Tammie	Teresa	Tillie
Basil	Oregano	Catnip	Cheese	Peanuts
French bread	Rye bread	Pita bread	White bread	Wheat bread
Lemonade	Ginger ale	Iced tea	Root beer	Grape juice

31. Family Confusion

Bess	Betty	Belinda	Bonnie	Barb
Byron Wu	Bill Jones	Bart Villars	Ben Doe	Bob Smith
Bill	Bart	Bob	Byron	Ben
Betty	Bess	Barb	Belinda	Bonnie

32. Halloween Fun

Peggy	Pauline	Patrick	Pierre	Phillip
Goat	Cow	Horse	Pig	Donkey
Pumpkin	Princess	Jockey	Ballerina	Pirate
Marshmallows	Chocolate	Gumdrops	Jellybeans	Licorice

33. Fishing Around

Sidney	Sara	Sal	Sammi	Shawn
1500 casts	1657 casts	1000 casts	500 casts	750 casts
Carp	Perch	Bass	Pike	Trout
2 pounds	1 pound	3 pounds	5 pounds	6 pounds

34. Dinner for Five

James	Jane	Jake	Janet	Joe
Seat 1	Seat 2	Seat 5	Seat 4	Seat 3
Bacon	Salami	Bologna	Cheese	Ham
Milk	Coffee	Tea	Cola	Water

35. Fair Enough

Elsbeth	Eliot	Erin	Eddie	Edith
10 pies	15 pies	20 pies	30 pies	37 pies
3rd place	2nd place	5th place	4th place	1st place
15 ears	20 ears	10 ears	37 ears	30 ears

© 2005 MindWare

36. Frog Frolics

Frank	Farrah	Faith	Fred	Phillip
15 flies	30 flies	5 flies	22 flies	10 flies
30 feet	10 feet	15 feet	5 feet	22 feet
22 croaks	5 croaks	30 croaks	10 croaks	15 croaks

37. School Science Fair

Deke	Dave	Diane	Daphne	Dale
Mr. Butler	Mr. Porter	Mrs. Skinner	Mrs. Blake	Ms. Spencer
5th place	4th place	3rd place	2nd place	1st place
String	Pulleys	Magnets	Doorbell	Volcano

38. Did You Drop That?

Hank	Harriet	Harold	Hester	Hiram
Pinkney	Smedley	Putney	Dixie	Snider
Hudson	Nash	Edsel	Desoto	Packard
Sprocket	Widget	Whatsis	Whosit	Thingie
Red	Pink	Orange	Yellow	Green

39. Catfish Complaints

Whiskers	Tabby	Tom	Bubbles	Fred
Frogs	Worms	Crawdads	Snails	Cheeseballs
Carp	Minnows	Bass	Eels	Fishermen
5 pounds	8 pounds	4 pounds	15 pounds	16 pounds
June	July	March	October	December

40. Everything's Relative

Max	Mark	Mike	Mickey	Martin
Godfrey	Greg	Gunther	Gale	George
Gail	Gina	Georgina	Greta	Gertrude

1st couple	2nd couple	3rd couple	4th couple	5th couple
George	Godfrey	Gale	Greg	Gunther
Greta	Georgina	Gertrude	Gail	Gina

41. Warthogs Cook

Wanda	Wendy	Winnie	Wilma	Winona
Portal	Snead	Slader	Stockley	Spreckley
1st place	2nd place	3rd place	5th place	4th place
Black apron	Red apron	Green apron	Yellow apron	Blue apron
4 hours	2 hours	3 hours	6 hours	7 hours

42. Movie Magic

Roman	Roland	Roger	Richard	Raymond
Wooley	Wolsey	Webber	Weeley	Wacker
Boston	Seattle	New York	Miami	Chicago
Yawntanic	Sinktanic	Dozetanic	Deeptanic	Wetanic
May	January	June	March	October

43. Did I Order That?

Elvira	Edward	Ernie	Ellie	Ernst
Perch	Shrimp	Steak	Chicken	Lobster
Spinach	Corn	Beets	Beans	Potatoes
Pie	Cake	Pudding	Ice cream	Tart
Milk	Lemonade	Tea	Cola	Coffee

44. Band of Gorillas

Gordon	Gayle	George	Gregory	Ginny
Bugle	Saxophone	Tuba	Trumpet	Trombone
Guitar	Banjo	Violin	Cello	Harp
Milli Gorilli	Spice Gorillas	The Whew	5 Ape Night	Apeful Dead
30 bananas	28 bananas	61 bananas	60 bananas	14 bananas

45. A New Show

Tom	Tess	Tillie	Toula	Terry
Keke	Kuku	Kiki	Kaka	Koko
Pink	Green	Blue	Purple	Orange
Bicycle	Skateboard	Scooter	Tricycle	Unicycle
"Bummer"	"Booboo"	"Boing"	"Babaloo"	"Bink"

46. It's News to Me

Biff	Betsy	Bonnie	Byron	Bill
Grant	Lincoln	Hayes	Wilson	Tilden
Boston	Chicago	New York	San Diego	Seattle
The Dispatch	The Tribune	The Times	The Globe	The Post
Politics	Crime	Entertainment	Sports	Finance

47. Educational Theory

Monday	Tuesday	Wednesday	Thursday	Friday
Math	English	History	Logic	Geography
Mr. Carter	Mr. Nixon	Mrs. Reagan	Mrs. Johnson	Mrs. Truman
Room 302	Room 301	Room 304	Room 306	Room 300
Black shoes	Yellow shoes	Brown shoes	Blue shoes	Red shoes

48. Early Achievements

Ooga	Egga	Ugga	Aaga	Iggy
Whysees	Whensees	Whosees	Whatsees	Wheresees
Shoes	Washing	Cooking	Stone axe	Underwear
Huts	Caves	Trees	Holes	Under rocks
Red	Yellow	Orange	Blue	Pink

49. Sun Safety

Jill	Jane	Joan	Jenny	Joanna
Spain	Aruba	Mexico	Bermuda	Florida
TanBest	TanOk	TanEz	Tanique	TanSafe
$4	$3	$5	$2	$10
Factor 30	Factor 10	Factor 40	Factor 5	Factor 35

50. Farm Errands

Bert	Betty	Belle	Brad	Ben
Polk	Adams	Grant	Taylor	Tyler
Potatoes	Tomatoes	Beans	Corn	Squash
Dentist	Haircut	Sick friend	Fertilizer	Seed
Pig	Cow	Goat	Goose	Duck

 © 2005 MindWare